MY DAD GOT HURT.
WHAT CAN I DO?

Helping

Military

Children

Cope with a

Brain-Injured

Parent

National Academy of Neuropsychology Foundation

With Brunella Costagliola

Illustrated by Valerio Mazzoli

First Edition

Copyright © 2017 National Academy of Neuropsychology Foundation

Interior Graphics Credit: Valerio Mazzoli

ISBN: 978-1-4834-7257-7 (sc)
ISBN: 978-1-4834-7258-4 (hc)
ISBN: 978-1-4834-7256-0 (e)

Library of Congress Control Number: 2017910804

Lulu Publishing Services rev. date: 07/28/2017

This book is brought to you by:
The National Academy of Neuropsychology Foundation
Promoting Neurowellness through Education

Acknowledgments

We would like to thank Susan and Jeff Jones, Dr. Jerid M. Fisher, and Steve and Rich Barnes for their generous underwriting of this project. Thank you, Karen Moyer, for permission to use the 7Cs in our book. Also, a special thanks to Brunella Costagliola and Valerio Mazzoli for their excellent work.

This book is dedicated to the brave men and women in uniform
who put their lives on the line every day for the rest of us.
Thank you for your service!

Dear Reader,

The National Academy of Neuropsychology Foundation is a nonprofit organization whose mission is to educate the public about brain injuries and the prevention of these disorders. We are very proud to present you with this book, which is a work of love, respect, and esteem for all the men and women who have selflessly chosen to serve our country.

The aim of this book is to help educate children who have a military parent who has sustained a brain injury. While brain injury is a complex topic, it is an unfortunate fact that certain types of brain injuries, which are all too common in our wounded warriors, affect a person's behaviors, such as mood and temper.

Often, a previously kind and loving parent may become irritable, short-fused, and intolerant of frustration after a brain injury. To a child, these changes can be scary and overwhelming. Children may not understand why Mom or Dad is so different and may blame themselves for their parent's moodiness.

We decided to share thoughtful lessons with these children about a brain-injured parent in the context of a fictional family story. The story introduces the concept of a combat-induced brain injury and discusses how this injury can adversely affect the brain and change behaviors.

Most importantly, this book offers the young reader a practical coping tool called the 7Cs. The 7Cs are meant to empower children to feel comfortable and confident about themselves in these difficult circumstances. By doing so, the child can become a more active participant in his or her injured parent's life.

Thank you,
The National Academy of Neuropsychology Foundation

Hi, everyone! My name is Dr. Johnson, and I would like to welcome you to my office.

Can you guess what kind of doctor I am? Let me give you a hint:
I study the brain and its functions. Interesting, right?

I am a neuropsychologist (nur-oh-sī-COL-oh-jist). Yes, I know,
it's a hard word to remember. But you can do it!

Well, now that you have gotten comfortable, I would
like to tell you a story. Are you ready?

Today, I will introduce you to the Smith family.

Meet Mom and Dad.

This is Jackson; he's nine years old.

And Isabella is seven.

Oh, and let's not forget their adorable dachshund, Sally! Isn't she sweet?

Dad is in the military. Is your mom or dad in the military as well? Wonderful! Then, this story may just be for you.

It all started when …

The Smith family lives on a military base. They have a big backyard, which is great because they all love to spend time outside!

Dad, Jackson, and Isabella have fun playing catch. Dad coaches the baseball team at school.

Meanwhile, Mom is busy with the barbeque. They are having hot dogs, hamburgers, and lots of veggies. Yummy! I can tell it smells delicious!

There truly is nothing better than spending quality time as a family!

Every day, Dad puts on his uniform before going to work.

However, today something is different. He also has a big green bag with him, all packed and ready to go.

"Daddy, why do you have to leave?" Isabella asks.

"I have to deploy, sweetheart. It's part of my job, and it is necessary to keep us all safe," Dad answers.

"Dad, when will you be back?" Jackson is curious.

"In six months, buddy."

"We will all miss you," Mom says.

After a big, squeezy hug, Mom, Jackson, Isabella, and Sally wave goodbye to Dad.

Six months is a very long time, and lots of things happen in the meantime.

Isabella and Jackson miss Dad very much. Sally seems to be a bit mopey, too.

At night, before going to sleep, they both get to have a goodnight kiss from the jar of goodnight kisses Dad prepared before deploying. It's a real treat!

Since Dad is at a location where he doesn't always have access to a phone or a computer, it's such a wonderful surprise when they get to see him on Skype.

Unfortunately, though, one day, Dad's Humvee is in an accident. The accident leaves Dad with a brain injury, and he has to spend a long time at a military hospital.

But a day brings another day and another day again.

And before they know it … tick … tock … it's time!

"Daddy is coming home today!" Jackson and Isabella are very happy.
They have lots of fun making posters to welcome Dad home!

On their way to the airport, both children can hardly contain their joy.

"I can't wait to play catch with him again!" Jackson says.

"And I can't wait to have a tea party with him again!" Isabella adds.

As soon as they see him, they run toward Dad, who is *finally home*!

Although everybody is excited to have Dad back, before long, Jackson and Isabella start to notice that something just doesn't seem quite right.

Dad is not his usual patient self …

"Dad, do you want to play catch with me?" Jackson asks.
But Dad doesn't seem to hear him …

He has also been very moody lately, and he seems to be upset all the time.

"Maybe he's mad at me because I didn't pick up all
my toys yesterday," Isabella whispers.

"Maybe he's mad at me because I didn't finish all
my veggies at lunch," Jackson says.

"Why is Dad yelling at Mom?" they ask.

Sally is sad too.

Today, Dad is busy with the baseball team; it's the big game against the rival school.

Jackson and his teammates do their best, supported by Isabella and the other cheerleaders. Even Mom and Sally are there to watch, cheering from the bleachers. But their opponents are just too strong, and they win the game.

"You're a bunch of good-for-nothing losers!" Dad shouts, running toward his team. He is very angry.

Jackson and his friends are very sad about their coach's reaction. Why is he behaving this way? He used to be so supportive and caring.

Jackson and Isabella are mortified.

"I just wish somebody could help us," Jackson whispers.

Not to worry, kids! Help is on the way!

"Hello, Jackson; hi, Isabella. Nice to meet you! I'm Dr. Johnson, and I am here to help you!"

"Hello, Dr. Johnson," Jackson and Isabella reply. "Thank you for meeting with us!"

"First of all, it's important to understand how the human brain works. So let's take a peek inside. The brain is divided into four different sections, or lobes, and what we want to focus on today are the frontal lobes."

"The frontal lobes are the 'boss' of the brain because they control so many things, all very important. We use our frontal lobes to *decide* what to eat for breakfast; we use them to *plan* our day, *remember* things and *control* our behavior. We also use them to *express* our emotions and personality. If someone hits his head very hard, he might damage his frontal lobes."

"That's what happened to our daddy. He was in an accident, and he hit his head very hard. But he doesn't have any scars—they are all gone!" Jackson says.

"Well, when we injure our brains, we don't always see cuts, scars, or scratches on the outside," Dr. Johnson says. "While Dad might look like his usual self on the outside, he still has a wound on the inside. I'll bet you've noticed that Dad doesn't act the same way he used to, does he?"

"No … he seems … angrier, and he doesn't think before speaking. He can be so rude and hurtful," Isabella says.

"That is because his injury is in the frontal lobes, and he is having a hard time controlling his behavior and expressing his emotions like he used to," explains Dr. Johnson.

"But if his injury is on the inside, how can we fix it?" Jackson asks.

"That's what doctors and medicines are for! We are all here to help Dad and your family get better," Dr. Johnson says. "And now, I have a present for you two!"

"A present? What is it?" Isabella asks.

"It's a poster to put up in your room! Look, these are called the 7Cs. It's important to remember them when you are sad or upset about Dad. I know you are confused about Dad's behavior, but you need to always keep in mind these things:

1. I didn't *cause* it.
2. I can't *control* it.
3. I can't *cure* it.
HOWEVER
4. I can take *care* of myself
5. By *communicating* my feelings,
6. By making good *choices*, and
7. By *celebrating* myself.

Dad's brain injury will take a long time to heal. He needs your understanding, love, and support. By using the 7Cs, you can help him as well as others!"

"Thank you, Dr. Johnson! You are our hero!" Jackson and Isabella shout happily.

"Mom, Dad! Look what we have!" Isabella says, showing them the 7Cs poster.

"Dr. Johnson explained everything that is happening to you, Dad. Don't worry; doctors will take great care of you, and we are here to help too!" Jackson explains.

"I have such a wonderful and loving family!" Dad says, giving them all a big, squeezy hug.

As for me, mission accomplished! On to my next adventure!

The End.

If you require assistance in finding a qualified neuropsychologist, contact the NAN Foundation at www.nanfoundation.org.

Biographies

The National Academy of Neuropsychology (NAN) Foundation is a nonprofit organization dedicated to educating people worldwide about brain injuries and other brain disorders. The NAN Foundation, with its special focus on neuropsychology, is uniquely able to provide information that may help prevent brain injuries as well as assist those who have a brain injury or brain disease to find ways to live more fulfilling, quality lives. We also assist the loved ones of those with brain injuries to understand the changes that may occur in the way a person thinks, acts, and behaves in the wake of brain damage. For more information, please visit: www.nanfoundation.org.

The Moyer Foundation is dedicated to providing comfort, hope, and healing to children and families affected by grief and addiction. Our innovative resources and programs address the critical needs of children experiencing powerful, overwhelming, and often confusing emotions associated with the death of someone close to them or substance abuse in their family. No child should have to face these struggles alone, and our unique programs bring kids together to ease their pain and provide the tools to help restore hope. For more information, please visit: www.moyerfoundation.org.

Jerid M. Fisher, Ph.D., ABN is a board-certified forensic neuropsychologist with more than thirty years of experience. In Fisher's role as the chairman of the National Academy of Neuropsychology Foundation, he is particularly interested in educating the children of our Wounded Warrior families. Fisher is a fellow of the American Board of Professional Neuropsychology, clinical associate professor of psychiatry at the University of Rochester Medical Center, and an adjunct assistant professor of clinical psychology at SUNY Albany. He has published multiple peer-reviewed articles, book chapters, and books, including the true crime story, *Upside Down: Madness, Murder, and the Perfect Marriage*. For more information, please visit: www.jeridfisher.com.

Brunella I. Costagliola is a best-selling editor, ghostwriter, and published author. She earned two master's degrees from the prestigious Leiden University, The Netherlands, and is a certified English teacher from the University of Cambridge, UK. Throughout her career, she has had the pleasure and honor of working alongside best-selling authors, award-winning authors, and everyday heroes. Her articles have been published by a wide variety of magazines, websites, and college books. She has also worked with well-respected and prominent publishing houses. She is a proud Air Force wife and mother to two wonderful children. For more information, please visit: www.brunellacostagliola.com.

Valerio Mazzoli has been a Disney cartoonist since 1970. In 1989, he was contacted by Walt Disney Company to build eleven attractions at Disneyland Paris, France, including the symbol of the park, the Sleeping Beauty Castle. He is the owner of Valerio Mazzoli Studios, where he continues to give rise to an ever-changing style and poetry that we enjoy in his works, which will forever transmit the feeling and sensations of his life commitment to art, dreams, imagination, and hope. He lives in Florida with his family. For more information, please visit: www.valeriomazzoli.com/wp/home.